A Guide for Sharing Your Faith

The Small Book on Small Group Evangelism

DR. JOHN R. SCONIERS, II

Scripture quotations created to NIV are from the Holy Bible, New International Version. Copyright © 1973, 1978, 1984, 2011 by Biblica, Inc. Used by permission. All rights reserved.

Scripture quotations marked "NKJV" are taken from the New King James Version. Copyright © 1982, by Thomas Nelson, Inc. Used by permission. All rights reserved.

Scripture quotations from The Authorized (King James) Version. Rights in the Authorized Version in the United Kingdom are vested in the Crown. Reproduced by permission of the Crown's patentee, Cambridge University Press

Scripture quotations marked ESV are from the ESV Bible (The Holy Bible, English Standard Version), Copyright © 2001 by Crossway, a publishing ministry of Good News Publishers. Used by permission. All rights reserved.

Printed in the United States of America

Library of Congress Control Number: 2022906191

ISBN-13: 979-8-9862047-0-3
ISBN-13: 979-8-9862047-1-0

Real Moments Media
1385 Wilmington Way Suite 100
Grayson, GA 30017
www.realmomentsmedia.com

Dedicated in memory of my father, John R. Sconiers, Sr., my wife, Nicole, my mom, Maybell, and my children. Thank You for your continued support and prayers in everything that is accomplished!

The fruit of the righteous is a tree of life, And one who is wise gains souls.

Contents

PREFACE ix

INTRODUCTION xi

CHAPTER 1. What Is Evangelism? 1

CHAPTER 2. What is Small Group Evangelism? 5

CHAPTER 3. Is Small Group Evangelism New? 11

Jesus in Small Groups with His Disciples 12

Small Groups in the Book of Acts. 16

Paul Ministering in Small Groups. 17

Numerical Growth as a Result of Small Group
Evangelism 17

Disciples, Discipleship and Evangelism. 18

Conclusion 18

CHAPTER 4. Principles of Small Group Evangelism 21

CHAPTER 5. Remember the Goal of Small Group Evangelism! .27

Discipleship and Growth 30

CHAPTER 6. Strategies For Small Group Evangelism? 35

CHAPTER 7. Small Group Evangelism Conclusions 41

CHAPTER 8. Example Plan For Small Group Evangelism. 45

Participants 46

Gathering and Events 46

ABOUT THE AUTHOR 57

CONNECT WITH DR. SCONIERS. 59

Preface

Though your beginning was insignificant,
Yet your end will increase greatly.

Job 8:7 NASB

"Everything has a beginning"

C hristian denominations generally have low growth rates and stagnant evangelistic programs. While churches struggle to evangelize new believers, evangelistic models that utilize small group methodology have shown various degrees of success. However, regardless of the methodology, utilizing small groups generally almost always leads to success. *The Small Book on Small Group Evangelism* seeks to define biblical principles of small groups that can help the reader introduce concepts that will help people grow their ministry numerically and/or personally in terms of their spiritual growth.

This work, *The Small Book on Small Group Evangelism*, started off with humble and simple beginnings. The original intent was to fulfill a small seminary project based on community evangelism and church growth. However, after performing minor research about small groups, there were several ideas and notions that intrigued me.

Later, as I pursued my doctoral studies, I was impressed by God that not only could research in the area of small group evangelism benefit me scholastically, but also I recognized its implementation in my ministry context would yield fruit. Hopefully the insights provided herein can assist you in developing strategic evangelistic programs based on the small groups evangelistic model presented. My prayer is that not only will you apply this information to your ministry settings, but also it will allow you to improve growth rates and member participation.

Introduction

The grass withers, the flower fades, But
the word of our God stands Forever!

Isaiah 40:8 NASB

"Challenged, but God is still with us!"

After his resurrection, Jesus Christ gave the
Great Commission in Matthew 28:16-20:

16 But the eleven disciples proceeded to Galilee, to the mountain which Jesus had designated. 17 When they saw Him, they worshiped Him; but some were doubtful. 18 And Jesus came up and spoke to them, saying, "All authority has been given to Me in heaven and on earth. 19 Go therefore and make disciples of all the nations, baptizing them in the name of the Father and the Son and the Holy Spirit, 20 teaching them to observe all that I commanded you; and lo, I am with you always, even to the end of the age. NASB

Jesus instructed His eleven remaining disciples and followers to evangelize and grow the church. However, to embark on this endeavor, Jesus promised the disciples they would receive supernatural assistance (John 14, Acts 2). On the day of Pentecost, the Holy Spirit descended upon the disciples. Peter, one of Jesus's eleven disciples, began to witness with boldness to the multitude who gathered. Peter hoped that the individuals' hearts would be pricked as their conscience brought on a feeling of guilt and remorse. When the multitude asked what they should do in response to Peter's witness, Peter replied that they should be baptized. That day, there were three thousand people baptized and added to the church (Acts 2:41). This would serve as the foundation of the New Testament church in which growth aided by the Holy Spirit almost immediately started. This growth was started by a small group of disciples but was explosive, and it "added to the church daily" (Acts 2:47). This initial act served as the springboard that would propel the New Testament Church forward to evangelize and create disciples in other parts of the known world, so all might know the good news of Jesus Christ.

The Acts of the Apostles in the New Testament serves as a dramatic and fascinating description of the history of the first Christian church after the resurrection of Jesus Christ to the Christian Church. The book of Acts of the Apostles describes what the Great Commission referenced, God's new work on earth did not end with the resurrection of Jesus Christ. The work continues through the Holy Spirit that pours out on faithful followers. The disciples would grow from a small, frightened group to become a dynamic movement with Spirit-given power to turn "the world upside down" (Acts 17:6). The disciples' work after Pentecost described in Acts and the epistles record additional information about church growth, evangelism, and small groups. These things are profoundly useful for church growth.

In today's church, the mission has not changed. The church is still attempting to go into the world and make disciples by declaring the good news of Jesus Christ under the power and urging of the

Holy Spirit to bring in new believers. Over the years, many churches across the country believe in evangelizing their community, so non-believers are aware of the Second Coming of Jesus Christ and their need to avail themselves of their only hope, Jesus Christ. This led churches to grow numerically and personally to participate in the mission to save souls. Today, growing the church numerically is still essential as it is still an outward indicator of the follow-through of the stated mission. However, most Christian churches today are either plateauing or declining. Is God stopping the church from growing because He seeks to discipline Her for not being faithful? No. The church remains stagnant because we have failed to implement biblical principles in evangelism. These principles would seem to include small groups, as even most individuals often would cite key verses including Acts 2:41-47 to establish the foundation for small group ministries.

While some church leaders acknowledge the importance of evangelism through small groups and biblical principles associated with it, they have yet to implement them into their churches actively. Many successful pastors have enjoyed sustained numerical growth in their ministries. Upon careful examination, they almost have used small groups exclusively at the center of their ministry often designing discipleship, worship, fellowship and other key launchpads from the concept. They believe that the small group's purpose is the same purpose of the church, which is spelled out in John 17:3. Specifically, the purpose of a small group's existence is to enable others to know God, and to allow God to be known. The formula for many successful ministries' evangelistic success is heavily dependent on small groups.

My belief is that small groups are not only biblical, but they are essential in the modern church. By looking at the book of Acts, you can see the extraordinary growth of the church and how they cared for and discipled them. It all started with small groups. Acts 2 is a clear description of small group evangelism in which new believers were able to "break bread in their homes and ate together with gladness of hearts" (Acts 2:46). The strategy of small groups led to exponential growth then, and it also can lead to exponential growth in your ministry.

The Christian church at large is genuinely in need of a solution for the continual demise of its stagnant evangelistic program and its inability to keep existing members in the pews. The church struggles to evangelize new believers and mobilize or keep its existing members. While the erosion of any church is generally a slow process that could take years, the inability to keep existing members, mobilize them in the community, and add new members means the church is in danger of becoming deceased. Small groups can provide the catalyst that propels substantial growth of the church, expands the Great Commission, and leads others to a relationship with Jesus Christ.

CHAPTER 1

WHAT IS EVANGELISM?

Go into all the world and preach the gospel to all creation.
Mark 16:15 NASB

"Go means Go! All means all!"

I f you ask five church members what evangelism is, you most
likely will get five different answers. To some, evangelism means
setting up a tent and holding a meeting where they talk about Jesus.
To others, it might be helping the poor and disenfranchised. To
others, evangelism means passing out literature about the Bible.
Many people will have an idea of things that might be associated
with evangelism, but they may not necessarily understand what
evangelism *is.*

The word, evangelism, comes from the Greek words *euaggelion,*
which means "a good message, or gospel" and *euaggelizo,* which
means "to announce, declare, bring, or preach this good news."
Those who practice evangelism are indeed delivering a message

— one of extraordinarily good news, life-giving and transformative power, and eternal ramifications. For our purposes, evangelism will be defined as "the sharing of the gospel by proclamation, acts of service, or any other means that gives people a chance to come into a personal relationship with Jesus Christ."

The gospel writers all rooted their story in evangelism or the message of Jesus Christ who came to Earth to deliver, teach, die, and rise again for all of us! Jesus wants everyone to spread the word. Jesus came so that we may live and have life more abundantly. Jesus wants people to know they can be part of God's Holy Kingdom and partake of everlasting life. He directs all His loyal followers to evangelize throughout Scripture.

In Matthew 28:19-20, Jesus tells us, "Therefore go and make disciples of all nations, baptizing them in the name of the Father and of the Son and of the Holy Spirit, and teaching them to obey everything I have commanded you. And surely I am with you always, to the very end of the age." We are to spread this good news everywhere — to the ends of the Earth. The sharing of the good news of Jesus Christ by proclamation, acts of service, or any means that gives individuals a chance to come into a personal relationship with Jesus Christ is evangelism! The hope of performing evangelism is to draw oneself and others to become more and more like Jesus Christ or enrich your relationship and closeness with Jesus Christ. The people with whom we are interacting not only include those in the community of believers, but also they include those who are unchurched and inactive. Inactive members would be those people who do not attend worship service regularly with the exception of commonly accepted general services like Easter, Christmas, weddings, or funerals. In the broader sense, being "unchurched" references people who identify as Christian but are not connected with a church. As of 2004, there were approximately 75 million people in the United States who were considered unchurched.

The Christian world often refers to evangelism as church growth because growth usually is achieved by evangelism. Church growth, generally identified as numerical and not spiritual, often eludes most churches. In a recent study, more than sixty percent of Protestant churches in the United States are identified as having plateaued or declining in attendance, and more than half of the remaining forty percent of Protestant churches saw less than ten people become new Christians in the past twelve months. The percentages are considerably worse for smaller churches that have a weekly attendance of one hundred members or fewer. While many pastors and laypersons point to resources, space limitations, and leadership as reasons for stagnation, when carefully examined, these failing churches usually are lacking formal or informal small group ministries. There are materials and conferences that church leaders can utilize to help facilitate evangelistic growth by utilizing various methodologies. However, evangelistic growth through small group ministries is generally overlooked. As a result, most churches do not effectively have small group ministries.

CHAPTER 2

WHAT IS SMALL GROUP EVANGELISM?

For where two or three are Gathered in
my name, there I am among them.

Matthew 18:20 NASB

"God is in the midst."

S mall group evangelism, especially in terms of small groups, is a complex and ever-expanding subject to be digested because there are multiple theories, methods, and notions. Several books, articles, journals, and thesis projects relating to church growth, evangelism, and small groups were reviewed by myself and were relevant to the field of small group evangelism. A small group within the church is a voluntary, intentional gathering of 3 to 12 people that regularly meets together with the shared goal of mutual Christian edification and fellowship. Usually, small groups meet for a specific length of time and about a specific topic. Small groups could be both formal and informal. For example, Sabbath School groups, choirs, Bible study participants, deacon boards, women groups, men's groups, couples' groups, etc. While each group meets for a specific reason or topic, they are smaller subsets of the overall church. Turning the small group into an evangelistic arm of the church simply requires meeting for evangelistic outreach with the goal of multiplying or discipling others. The group should continue to function as a part of a local church, not as an independent entity.

When a small group within the church outwardly shares the gospel by proclamation, acts of service, or any means that gives people a chance to come into a personal relationship with Jesus Christ, they are performing small group evangelism. The group arranges their lives around improving their ability to perform outreach in the community. The big idea is for the individuals within the small group to come together with the sole purpose of presenting the gospel in an outward fashion. Without the outward fashion, usually, evangelism is not the goal.

Small groups can be defined in various ways. Some definitions suggest that small groups consist primarily of church members and should not go beyond twelve people because not only is that the number of Jesus's disciples, but also adding more than twelve people will decrease the effectiveness of the small group gradually. This approach would subdivide the group if it ever grew to more than twelve people. Others generally have arrived at the conclusion that a small group should be between six and twenty people. The author of this text has seen small groups range from four to thirty-five or more people and believes the actual size of the small group doesn't matter. What does matter is for the group to be manageable by its leader and still provide valuable interaction among participants. If the group ever becomes unmanageable, the small group should split into more manageable chunks with new leaders emerging.

Regardless of the size of the group, purpose is what drives a small group. The small group within the church is a voluntary and intentional gathering, regularly meeting together with the shared goal of mutual Christian edification and fellowship. In order to be effective, the small group must come together regularly for a common purpose and progress toward Christ. The common purpose within the group should be driven by the group's leadership and agreed on by all parties. Anyone who doesn't agree with the purpose should spawn a new small group with like minded individuals. Through its common purpose, spiritual enlightenment and fellowship along with evangelistic outreach to multiply the body of Christ are the goals of the group.

Usually, there is a specific length of time the small group meets that is incorporated into its charter. The charter describes why the small group was created and what is its sole driving function. For instance, the group's purpose may be literature evangelism, feeding the homeless, etc. As long as the group includes God and stays centered on its charter, the small group can function as needed and not turn into a social club. Following these principles allows the small group to be the driving force behind evangelism and church growth.

In many cases, the small group becomes a community within the community of believers of the church. The term "community" has its roots in Latin and means "common," "public," or "shared by all or many." A community is a unified group of people who engage or embrace ordinary circumstances, beliefs, values, and differences. There is a great need for communities and relationships in today's culture due to the interconnectedness of society through social media platforms, cross information sharing, and interest groups. While there may not be a connection or relationship between people, social media has connected individuals on a broader spectrum. Thus, connectivity and relationship is natural, implied, intuitive and part of every day life. There is a clear desire for community and closeness that can be provided effectively by small group engagement. Even large corporations attempt to boost profits and their bottom line by engaging in small group communities.

Connected small group communities are the life-long blood of churches, and in some ways, they were previously organically driven. Small group communities are places where community needs are met by love and support. The community effectively assists in a single need area such as grief recovery and establishes a support system. The community deals with the temporary need and brings individuals together to rally around those who have been affected. The small group acts as a place of community that provides love, friendship, fellowship, and discipleship. By forming a community within the community, the small group has additional privileges and advantages that others within the church do not. The small groups live in a relationship and enjoy meaningful friendship and encouragement. In a regular church service, people may visit one another before or after service, but this barely meets the definition of fellowship. There is little to no warmth, caring, sharing, or healing. However, when people are involved in the comfortable, non-threatening atmosphere of a small group, the same individuals not only receive the items missing from church fellowship but also openly discuss and fellowship in a more meaningful way.

Many Christian authors emphasize that forgiveness and reconciliation can be fostered more easily while in the community of a small group than in larger settings. Many who struggle with forgiving individuals find it difficult to talk about the situation with large groups of people, but in small groups, they feel safe, and they feel that they can talk about their hurts, problems, and healing. Think about small groups that engage in therapy or a mission to heal like Alcoholics Anonymous. The small groups are essentially the church community, but because it is a smaller segment of the church, it has exceptional influence and power in reconciliation. We should encourage churches to utilize small groups to be healing centers that allow all topics without boundaries. Therefore, they will allow individuals to be shaped and healed like the grafting of a limb to a plant.

Due to cultural dynamics, small groups are driven purposely to be sustained. These smaller subsets of church communities are connected by what they do for each other and what they do for others outside their community. The communities created by small groups allow individuals to connect inside them and receive the healing that embraces their engagement and fosters an environment of acceptance. There must be a stronger emphasis on how to revitalize these communities within the church because there is still a need to continue to develop communities of small groups within churches in which individuals can lock arms on their journey in modern times.

The church is composed of people who have decided to give their lives to Christ. Smaller subsets of the church gather in a variety of settings including worship. Other meetings of the church comprise subgroups called small groups. When these small groups revolve around outward ministry, the natural byproduct is numerical growth. If small groups are implemented in churches, the churches' numerical or spiritual growth rates will increase. If the purpose of the church is to evangelize according to the Great Commission, the church should be able to grow utilizing small groups. Most current research suggests the implementation of small groups fosters numerical and spiritual growth. The secondary issue of providing healing and fellowship will spring forth naturally as well.

CHAPTER 3

IS SMALL GROUP EVANGELISM NEW?

And they devoted themselves to the apostles' teaching and the fellowship, to the breaking of bread and the prayers. And awe[d] came upon every soul, and many wonders and signs were being done through the apostles. And all who believed were together and had all things in common. And they were selling their possessions and belongings and distributing the proceeds to all, as any had need. And day by day, attending the temple together and breaking bread in their homes, they received their food with glad and generous hearts, praising God and having favor with all the people. And the Lord added to their number day by day those who were being saved.

Where two or three are Gathered in my name, There I am among them

Acts 2:42-47 ESV

"Let the teaching and fellowship begin."

This chapter suggests a theological foundation for the scriptural mandate for growth developed in small groups. Several theological approaches are crucial to the issues of church growth, particularly concerning small groups. The Bible offers several examples that illustrate the importance of organizing God's people into small groups. However, the most significant examples concerning numerical church growth come from the New Testament where several stories about soul winning through small groups exist.

JESUS IN SMALL GROUPS WITH HIS DISCIPLES

The New Testament demonstrates the actions of the ministry of Jesus Christ from the beginning when He called twelve disciples for His ministry. In the three synoptic Gospels of Matthew, Mark, and Luke, the twelve disciples constituted a small group. Jesus called this small group to spread the gospel into the entire world. He started by calling four fishermen, followed by a tax collector. Then, Jesus appointed seven others.

Jesus went up on a mountainside and called to Him those He wanted, and they came to Him. He appointed twelve that they might be with Him, so He could send them out to preach and have authority to drive out demons. These are the twelve He appointed: Simon (to whom He gave the name Peter), James son of Zebedee and his brother John (to them, He gave the name Boanerges, which means "sons of thunder"), Andrew, Philip, Bartholomew, Matthew, Thomas, James son of Alphaeus, Thaddaeus, Simon the Zealot, and Judas Iscariot, who betrayed him (Mark 3:15-19; NIV, see also Matt 10:1-4; Luke 6:12-16).

Jesus knew the importance of small groups, and He understood the purpose of ministering in the context of small groups through His disciples. Jesus appointed twelve, designating them as apostles that they might live in a community with Him and be sent to evangelize others. Many disciples followed Jesus, but He chose the twelve apostles as the small group who could accomplish His mission. Jesus could have chosen more people, but instead, he kept the group limited in size. Before sending out His disciples on their first mission, Jesus spent time teaching and training them. Jesus also knew of the importance of support, so He did not send them out alone but divided them into smaller groups of two: "Calling the Twelve to him, he began to send them out two by two and gave them authority over impure spirits" (Mark 6:7, 12-13).

Often, Bible readers see Jesus meeting with the disciples and teaching them throughout His ministry. Jesus regularly ate with His disciples and encouraged open dialogue. This also occurs during the last supper when He asked the disciples to eat the bread and drink the cup until His Second Coming, so they would remember what He had done for them. "For I received from the Lord what I also passed on to you: The Lord Jesus, on the night he was betrayed, took bread, and when he had given thanks, he broke it and said, 'This is my body, which is for you; do this in remembrance of me.' In the same way, after supper he took the cup, saying, "This cup is the new covenant in my blood; do this, whenever you drink it, in remembrance of me." For whenever you eat this bread and drink this cup, you proclaim the Lord's death until he comes" (1 Cor. 11:23-25).

During other times Jesus sent out the twelve or a larger group of disciples (the seventy-two) for evangelism. Jesus knew the importance of what an evangelistic small group effort could do versus using a bigger group. Jesus sent seventy-two disciples out on a mission trip two by two. "After this, the Lord appointed seventy-two others and sent them two by two ahead of him to every town and place where he was about to go. He told them, "The harvest is plentiful, but the workers are few. Ask the Lord of the harvest, therefore, to send out workers into his harvest field" (Luke 10:1, 2).

Jesus and His disciples continued to study, pray, eat, and minister together in an evangelistically centered small group. Jesus was also with various disciples in small groups at different homes. These home meetings played a significant role in the rise of the early church, and some of the most quoted interactions happened within them. One of the essential things about small groups occurring within homes is that they develop deep relationships among the members. Notice the following activities involved in small gatherings and small group activities: Jesus prayed in a small group (Mark 14:32-41); Jesus ate dinner in a house with tax collectors and sinners (Matt. 9:10-13; Mark 2:15-17; Luke 5:29-32); Jesus was at Bethany in the house of Simon the leper (Matt. 26:6-13; Mark 14:3-9; John 12:1-8); Jesus healed a paralytic in his home (Matt. 9:2-8; Mark 2:1-12); Jesus healed many persons at Simon Peter's house (Matt. 8:14-17; Mark 1:29-34; Luke 4:38-41); Jesus stayed at the home of Zacchaeus, the tax collector (Luke 19:1-10); Jesus visited Martha and Mary in their home (Luke 10:38-42); Jesus forgave a sinful woman at the Pharisee's home (Luke 7:36-50).

In summary, in the small group experiences that Jesus had with His disciples, certain themes can be observed: The group met in the homes of group members, and they became part of a new family (Mark 1:29; 2:15; 3:31-34; 6:1-16). Jesus healed a group member's relative and sent out the group to heal and cast out evil spirits (Mark 1:30-31; 5:1-13; 6:7-13; 16:7); occasionally, the group lived with Jesus in isolated places (Mark 1:35-37; 1:45); and officials questioned the group about their activities and behavior (Mark 2:16). The group lived under constant scrutiny and criticism (Mark 2:18; with large expectant crowds; 3:7-10). The group shared the message and ministry of Jesus, but sometimes failed in their mission to spread the gospel (Mark 3:13-15; 6:30; 9:17-29; 9:38-41). The group often went hungry because of a lack of space or time to eat

(Mark 3:20). The individuals in the group were taught secrets that the crowd could not bear to hear (Mark 4:10); the group often lived in danger, fear, and conflict and was accused of breaking the law (Mark 2:24; 4:37-38; 7:5-12; 8:31-33; 10:13-16).

The group experienced the power of Jesus over the elements and the power of the Holy Spirit (Mark 4:39-41; 11:13-25; 14:32-34; 14:43-48; Acts 1:8). The group left villages and regions to feed large crowds with few resources and to maintain confidentiality with Jesus (Mark? 5:17; 6:37; 8:30). The group shared in rigorous travel (Mark? 5:21). The group coped with Jesus's intense sense of reality (Mark 5? 30-34). The group was called away by Jesus to rest (Mark? 6:31); the group was sent out alone without Jesus (Mark 6? 45). The group was shocked by Jesus's surprising words and actions (Mark? 6:49-50). The group missed the point of Jesus's teaching (Mark? 7:17-19).

The group served the crowd at the direction of Jesus (Mark 8:6-8); the group entered into dialogue and discussion and answered questions posed by Jesus (Mark 8: 16, 27). The group asked Jesus for insight about how to heal others (Mark 9:28-29). The group was often alone when taught by Jesus, and they often misunderstood His teachings (Mark 9:31-32; 9:35-37; 10:23-26). The group argued about who was the best leader next to Jesus (Mark? 9:33-34; 10:35-45; 14:10, 11). The group did theological reflections with Jesus (Mark 10:10); the group was surprised with Jesus's direction (Mark 10: 32). Jesus directed the group members to perform specific actions and say specific words (Mark 11:1-6). The group participated in learning processes with Jesus (Mark 13:1-4). The group engaged in observation and reflection with Jesus (Mark 13: 1-4). The group prepared for and participated in special celebrations (Mark: 14:12-16). The group regularly ate together, experienced difficulties together, and sang together (Mark: 14:18; 14:22-25). Jesus confronted the group with the truth about themselves, the world, and their lack of truth, loyalty, and faithfulness (Mark 14:16-

21; 14:27-31; 16:14). The group fell asleep in the middle of Jesus's most difficult emotional pain (Mark 14:35-41) and deserted Jesus when he was arrested (vs. 50-72).

SMALL GROUPS IN THE BOOK OF ACTS

The book of Acts describes various kinds of activities by the apostles as they worked to fulfill the Great Commission. The Holy Spirit was with the small group of apostles, assisting them to convert many people to Christianity. The New Testament book of Acts addresses the importance of evangelistic small groups and mentions that many of the early experiences took place in small groups within homes (or the upper room): the commissioning of the apostles (Acts 1:8); replacing Judas (1:15-26); giving the gift of tongues (Acts 2); organization of new churches (6:1-8); spreading the gospel beyond its original cultural, national, and racial groups (Acts 10); and changing church practices (Acts 10). During the New Testament era, there were often small group gatherings that met in private homes. During that time, Christians used the temple and their houses for prayer meetings (Acts 2:41; 5:42). The conversion of Lydia and her household most likely took place in her home (Acts 16:14, 15). The Philippian jailer and his family were converted in their home (Acts 16:23-32). Paul repeatedly refers to house churches and their meetings (Rom. 16:3-5; Col. 4:15; Acts 2:46; 12:12; Phil. 2). Small groups in the book of Acts and their meetings in homes were important in the New Testament for worship, teaching, fellowship, breaking bread, prayer, and devising evangelistic strategies. Small group meetings in homes and other places outside the temple provided a dynamic setting for fellowship, worship, and of course, evangelism. They were natural places that enabled Christians to gather and share their faith with nonbelievers. As a result, God added daily to their number.

PAUL MINISTERING IN SMALL GROUPS

In Paul's evangelistic journeys, he worked with Priscilla, Aquila, and Barnabas. These four people formed an evangelistic small group for ministry in which everyone was free to use his or her talents in God's work. Paul, Priscilla, and Aquila worked together in reaching many areas with the gospel. They preached the good news in synagogues, established new churches, and visited new groups of believers—all steps that make sense in the area of church growth. With Barnabas, Bible readers see God choosing people for His mission. Acts 13:1-3 is an example of the role played by the Holy Spirit in selecting a person for the mission. The Holy Spirit appointed Paul and Barnabas for God's work. Together, they were the core of an evangelistic small group that followed God's direction in leading new believers to Christ. Their small group evangelism led to an evangelistic growth rate that in today's terms would not only be successful, but extraordinary.

NUMERICAL GROWTH AS A RESULT OF SMALL GROUP EVANGELISM

After the disciples were filled with the Holy Spirit, they began to spread the good news everywhere. As a result, the church grew. Acts 1:15 establishes that there were 120 disciples in the upper room. After that, God added 3,000 new converts (Acts 2:41, 42), and soon, 5,000 men were numbered as believers (4:4). Acts 5:14 discusses how more and more people were believing, and the number of believers increased (Acts 6:1, 7; 9:3). The churches were planted (16:5), and many thousands committed their lives to Jesus (21:20). Luke's description of the numerical growth of the church is scattered through Acts. As readers follow the pattern of Acts 1:8, the church traces this growth beginning in Jerusalem (2:47; 4:4; 6:1, 7), and it spread through Judea and Samaria (9:31; 12:24) into the uttermost parts of the Earth (16:5; 19:20). Seemingly, the spread was due to the evangelistic power of small groups. A small group in the church facilitates new additions and influences many souls to come to the Lord. Churches see this play out again and again even when coming together as a small group to perform the mundane things like distributing food to Hellenistic widows. God used that small group in action to complete a simple task to bring about spiritual results that the number of disciples multiplied greatly in Jerusalem.

DISCIPLES, DISCIPLESHIP AND EVANGELISM

Jesus Christ makes it plain that the central focus of the New Testament Church is to make disciples of others by going and teaching all that they have been commanded to reach (Matthew 28:20). As such, the effectiveness of any Christian effort such as evangelism can be measured in the spiritual maturing of members and the creation of new followers. This requires the church to invest directly in the spiritual formation of its members which nurtures those who are believers and seeks new believers through acts of evangelism. While individuals are responsible for their own spirituality and use of the talents God gives them, Paul clearly outlines the church as being responsible for its performance in the disciple-making process (Ephesians 4:11-13).

CONCLUSION

The study of biblical small group evangelism or evangelistic small groups in New Testament churches' establishes a wealth of examples. Small group evangelism was important to the growth and development of the New Testament church as well as the surrounding communities. God has utilized, functioned within, and had a purpose for small group evangelistic ministries in the Bible and continues to want them to function today. The New Testament church of today has a responsibility to assist others in training, spiritual development, and the discipling of others.

The theology of small group evangelism should inform our present-day methodology. The church consists of small groups: families that come together to form a larger group that is broken down into evangelistic ministry groups based on connections. Evangelism is designed to be the focus of the church at large and in small ministry groups. Small group evangelism is the core of the church and should be the basis of its evangelistic thrust.

CHAPTER 4

PRINCIPLES OF SMALL GROUP EVANGELISM

And let us consider how to stir up one another to love and good works, not neglecting to meet together, as is the habit of some, but encouraging one another, and all the more as you see the Day drawing near.

Hebrews 10:24-25 ESV

"Start Stirring."

T he term, "disciple," originates from the Greek word, *mathētēs*, which refers to a learner or follower who is committed to a significant master. A disciple is a dedicated follower of Jesus Christ who adheres to biblical teachings and not only believes in but also works to hasten the second coming of Jesus Christ by spreading the gospel and being a living sacrifice. Disciples also are considered to be members of a church in which they regularly attend. This term refers to the journey of becoming or continuing to be a disciple. It is the process by which a disciple grows in Jesus Christ and is equipped by training, knowledge, faith, and the power and presence of the Holy Spirit to overcome the pressures and trials for the present life to become more like Christ.

One of the main themes observed in various literature is the evangelistic capacity that small groups have when they are formed and utilized correctly. In the 1920s and 1930s, Calvary Episcopal Church in New York City was one of the first to utilize small groups and small group principles formally with the specific purpose of engaging unbelievers. While Calvary Episcopal Church's usage of small group evangelism is perceived as the key to growing their church over the next thirty years, the small group movement is viewed as an underground movement that is more suitable for outside organizations or parachurch groups, which are faith-based organizations that work outside the denomination to engage in social welfare and evangelism. In the 1960s, small groups developed through anti-establishmentarianism with individuals seeking to evangelize without the use of forms, structures, or large-scale events. The small group movement in the early sixties increased in popularity mainly because of this paradigm shift and the evolving the way that churches saw themselves as a dynamic community. Their process of full commitment to Christ and one another propelled their outreach into places they had not visited previously. Over the last thirty years, there has been another significant movement towards small group evangelism to ensure churches seek, understand, and harness the efficiency of small groups. Unlike before, the mainstream church is leading the charge of utilizing small group evangelism to further the cause of God.

Small groups are the perfect place for evangelism. Although small groups may be small in size, their impact in terms of collaboration is highly effective. These dynamics provide interaction among both believers and nonbelievers who have not yet committed their lives to Jesus Christ. Small groups have an overwhelming effect of fostering secure connections and community bonds that otherwise would not exist. These bonds create an environment that is non-threatening and provide an opportunity for people to connect in a natural way to form relationships and feel comfortable in asking questions. As these bonds are established within the given community, the dynamics bring unity of thought and action. Many churches have found that evangelism from small groups will increase our capacity to reach more people. When Christians follow the biblical method of small group evangelism, they are more likely to evangelize in relationship with other disciples than evangelizing in isolation. Too often, Christians focus on an individualized approach to Christianity, but Christianity is designed to share in community like a meal. Group members of a small group intend to participate with Christ in building His ever-expanding kingdom in the hearts of individuals who are within the small group and believers in the world. The bonds that are developed are strengthened by an atmosphere that allows integration that is difficult to accomplish in an individualized or larger setting. A small group can centralize the focus of emotion, energy, time, and effort towards one goal. By mixing existing members with new members and inviting them into a personal setting, a small group provides intergenerational and intercultural opportunities that foster shared experience and growth. This overarching dynamic is yearned for by new and existing members of the small group. Believing Christians want to be part of a group in which the goal is not knowledge or application but a personal and external transformation that connects other individuals with truth. This dynamic permits small groups to experience a connectedness that is difficult to achieve in a larger setting and is difficult to obtain on an individual basis. This type of connection creates a shift in thinking that leads small groups to have a more significant impact than any other evangelistic endeavor.

With small groups working together in the proper evangelistic mindset, others will connect with the small group community, and continue a relationship with God. This type of engagement will be encouraged to follow wholeheartedly after the Lord. Members of the group will feel drawn to participate actively regardless of their role or status. Thus, the groups tend to bond together to survive as a living collective, and they are able to overcome obstacles and impediments together.

Small groups are flexible and can adapt to all types of situations and minister in many different settings and ways. There is an emphasis on small groups' abilities by developing a litany of examples. Chief among them is their ability to engage and teach the new believer how to study the Bible, how to pray, and how to witness. Jesus recognized a small group approach as a way to accomplish His mission, and not utilizing small groups effectively means that individuals are rejecting biblical counsel. It is God's plan and Jesus's desire for Christians to grow in small groups. Small groups are places in which people can share their life in Christ and receive affirmation and discipleship. We are able to link Christ's ability to interest, attract, and maintain new believers directly to small groups. The fact is notable that by involving Bible interests in a small group before a nonbeliever joins the group, Jesus solved His retention problem and assimilated new members to biblical truth and doctrine.

Along the same lines and thought process, we can declare that small groups are foundational to the structure and success of the New Testament Church and the church of today. Small groups provide opportunities that allow individuals to minister to each other, utilize their spiritual gifts, and grow together based on their understanding of the New Testament Church's usage of small groups and the ways they assist in the development of spiritual gifts. The growth of spiritual gifts is considered an essential factor for developing small groups. The use of small groups helped those early church members develop their spiritual gifts. To facilitate the use and development of spiritual gifts within church members and operating within churches, small groups must be called upon to complete this mission. Otherwise, the church will fail to mobilize the power of the Holy Spirit, which would facilitate growth numerically and spiritually. Spiritual gifts build others up to be a blessing to the church and to help unbelievers establish a saving relationship with Jesus Christ. Small groups that form and engage in evangelistic activity are empowered by the Holy Spirit.

Small group leadership is essential because small groups need strong leadership that works in conjunction with church leadership in leading the congregation. The congregation will react based on the style of these leaders. For example, a pastor who is not engaged in the community will ignite separation in the community. Likewise, a small group leader not engaged with the church or its overall mission will also cause separation. Leaders should be sound doctrinally and able to command the respect of others while staying safely under the umbrella of the church.

Another area of importance for small groups is their transformative power. Multiple authors believed that small groups have the power to change lives. Small groups have an innate ability to disciple and encourage biblical truth to intersect with humanity and human relationships. At Willow Creek Community Church, small groups are the core organizational strategy that allows the transformation of character mind and soul. They become vehicles to reach each other and the lost world, bringing individuals into the subjection of Jesus Christ.

CHAPTER 5

REMEMBER THE GOAL OF SMALL GROUP EVANGELISM!

Rather, speaking the truth in love, we are to grow up in every way into him who is the head, into Christ, from whom the whole body, joined and held together by every joint with which it is equipped, when each part is working properly, makes the body grow so that it builds itself up in love.

Ephesians 4:15-16 ESV

"Grow up in Christ!"

Evangelism is a significant theme of thriving churches. While the importance of evangelism to thriving churches should seem natural, evangelism is a culture motivated by a desire to live life with the purpose that God requires and to save as many people as possible. As a church becomes mature and centered around God and the hope of Jesus Christ, there becomes an internal longing to tell others about the good news of Jesus Christ. This longing is like "fire shut up in one's bones" (Jeremiah 20:9) that compels the believer not to want to see anyone unaware or to see anyone perish.

There is a correlation between the emotional maturity of a church and its evangelistic thrust. If a church or individual proclaims to be a Christian but lacks passion for souls, that indicates a lack of spiritual maturity. Passion for souls exudes from the belief that evangelism and discipleship are the most crucial aims of Christianity. The believer accepts the Great Commission as a commandment and performs at the urging of the Holy Spirit.

The challenge to go out and disciple others compels the church to move forward as it becomes the motivating factor by which believers live and are judged. The church's mission of discipleship paves the way for its members and others with whom they are in contact to become active followers of Jesus Christ. Churches that are not mature seemingly have a form of Godliness, but they deny the power thereof as they try to be a Christian without true discipleship.

The mission draws a line of distinction where without believers fulfilling the mission to which Jesus Christ called everyone, there are no such things as being a Christian or Christianity. The thought of being a Christian without fulfilling the mission Christ called you to fulfill is lunacy. As the word, Christian, is derived from Christ and cannot exist on its own, the church is not a church without the mission of discipleship. This mission is paramount and should be at the forefront. While small groups are great, churches should not become enamored with small groups devoid of the mission. Some churches have fallen into the trap of forming small groups while attempting to be cultural or seeker sensitive, but the mission of reaching the lost should be at the forefront. Methods can change, but the mission stays the same. If the mission changes, and the church is not actively seeking the lost, then the church becomes no more than a social club. The problem with churches like this is that they have missed their mission to go, teach, and baptize.

Small groups, as well as the churches themselves, need to be intentional. Churches and their members should bathe themselves in prayer. However, even the prayer should be intentional. The church has been weakened severely by unintentional prayer that is more about people praying than about God or the people not in worship. Our prayer should be intentional, and this includes prayer for the Holy Spirit and the Holy Spirit's help in guiding, planning, and serving as evangelistic ambassadors of God. By being intentional in the evangelistic strategies of the church, the church will emphasize being biblically sound and seeking to grow the kingdom of God through new converts. After all, sin has created a gap between man and God. While Christ has filled that void and reconciled people to Him, the church should be a bridge to heavenly things that intentionally points others to Christ. When the church intentionally engages in this type of bridge-building, the resulting evangelistic thrust becomes more effective and far-reaching. The priorities of the church revolve around matters not focused on winning souls. Some churches are more concerned about the design of building or the makeup of the service. The church's lack of intentional evangelism and self-centered mindset represent a significant failing that, in essence, is idol worship.

Small groups that are outwardly focused and evangelistic are thriving in many churches. Individuals accomplish this in the small group by experiencing the connectedness of other individuals to accomplish what the early New Testament Church was able to accomplish. In today's world, small groups are the primary option for disciple-making and outward-facing growth because they allow direct individual evangelism in loosely formed organic structures. This methodology is strategic and is depicted in scripture.

When looking at evangelism in small groups, a key component for their usage is success in congregations in terms of growth and development. The first step is to understand that the task of the church and subsequently, its members is not to convert people but to witness to them about Christ. Christians should not view conversion as the mark of a fruitful witness. The church's engagement in witnessing is an indicator of success, regardless of the method utilized. The church has not failed if it has explained the gospel of Jesus Christ, and it has been rejected. Conversion is required for a sinner, but conversion is a function of genuine faith, which is given by the Holy Spirit and not by man. Evangelism, at its core, is teaching the gospel and intending to persuade one, while not taking into account success or failure. If conversion takes place, the church rightly should give credit to the Holy Spirit, so the church won't boast and believe that it is the reason for conversion.

DISCIPLESHIP AND GROWTH

At the basis of evangelism and church growth is discipleship. Jesus calls those who would follow Him to abandon all Earthly desires, even their family. As individuals pick up the mantle to follow Jesus Christ, they instantly become justified; however, there is a process of sanctification that requires a lifetime. While justification is a declarative and instantaneous process, sanctification is a transformative process of the character and condition of the individual. This means that it's an individual matter of progression for people after they profess their relationship with Christ because they may be at various spiritual levels. This progression, referred to as discipleship, is where one takes on the characteristics of Christ as empowered by conviction and the Holy Spirit. This is the aim of all Christians. Other contemporary Christian authors believed that without discipleship or the progression of individuals' Christian character, there truly is no Christ in the Christian.

The Church's main goal as instructed by Jesus Christ is to multiply intentionally through the means of disciple making and discipleship. Discipleship grows the individual into greater maturity in Christ as well as points to the same individual to be a witness of the gospel to others. Discipleship shows continual spiritual growth in four stages: conversion, basic spiritual growth, missionary mindedness, and the leader trainer stage. There should be a well-organized plan for the upbuilding of churches including training Christians how to conduct the work required for winning new souls to the kingdom and actually sending individuals out to experience the work firsthand.

However, many people today believe that the modern-day church is failing at making true disciples and assisting members in their spiritual growth. Instead, churches and their members have replaced discipleship with simple attendance, and they embrace values and ideas that are unbiblical and contradictory to the gospel. Not only are churches failing to disciple others, but they must come to the conclusion that discipleship can be better achieved by utilizing small groups. This view leads us to the fact that growth should not only occur in terms of numbers from baptisms, but growth should occur in one's personal life and the numbers of those participating in small groups.

Many of the problems that emerge in churches that fail to execute evangelism can be linked directly to the membership. The membership of most churches may attend church but spend little to no time each day seeking to become better acquainted with God. There is no daily devotion, prayer, or seeking to spend time one-on-one with God. There is a struggle for the members' time. It generally is allocated to work, family, and recreation rather than getting better acquainted with God. How can one who struggles with seeking to acquaint himself with God better lead others to Christ?

Simply stated, it is impossible. One must personally understand and experience the concept of peace that is offered through fellowship with Christ to want to lead someone else to the same peace. When there is a disconnect between a Christian and God, evangelism cannot take priority, and a problem ensues. The disconnect between a professed believer and God also plays into a growing theme in which individuals consider themselves spiritual, which in their minds makes them Christian even if they are not attempting to develop a relationship with God.

There are negative factors that can impact small groups. If structured carelessly, small groups can hinder growth, exclude people from participation, and provide platforms for harmful or destructive impacts. Although not emphasized in the biblical texts, most researchers would agree collectively that proper training and strong group dynamics are critical to the health of small groups. For small groups to succeed and achieve their goals, there must be intentional design, care, and feeding. Due to the absence of these components, small groups can damage the church and hinder the work of evangelism by causing strife and division.

Small groups must be intentional in recruiting as well as including the processes for directing and joining in a simplified manner. The rationale is that there must be an atmosphere that fosters camaraderie and vulnerability. The planning and execution of a group should be intentional but organic to foster the needed chemistry and remain faithful to this process to avoid pitfalls. There will be mistakes that cause issues among small groups; however, the importance of reducing these errors in leading and focusing on fostering healthy small groups is essential for its success.

There are also issues within small groups that appear to be cultural. These issues include creating groups consisting of couples and reaching men who are both married and single. There also are logistical issues like providing childcare, limiting group sizes, and recruiting leaders. These groups generally suffer for various reasons that exist outside the norm. Small group communities based on couples typically struggle with being open and vulnerable or opening up in front of their spouse. Men's groups plummet typically because of their lack of commitment. The logistical struggles mentioned may appear easy to overcome; however, they destroy most small groups before these groups form. Cultural norms, logistics, and other challenges should be taken into consideration when creating and facilitating small groups.

CHAPTER 6

STRATEGIES FOR SMALL GROUP EVANGELISM?

Take care, brothers, lest there be in any of you an evil, unbelieving heart, leading you to fall away from the living God. But exhort one another every day, as long as it is called "today," that none of you may be hardened by the deceitfulness of sin. For we have come to share in Christ, if indeed we hold our original confidence firm to the end.

Hebrews 3:12-14 ESV

"Exhort each other every day!"

S mall group evangelism allows people with similar objectives to point towards the same direction in a faith based endeavor.

They are allowed to share their beliefs and become acquainted with each other forming a bond of togetherness. The act of meeting is an essential entity in this setting. These people are unified towards the common goal, which lays the foundation of their relationship. The problems faced together, breakthroughs experienced while living, and small or large victories endured as a group are all crucial for the forward movement of these people. A small group is helpful in bringing people together who have a common objective in life. It helps them testify about what they have endured in life and in doing so, they can share how they have maintained their path in following their faith.

Most believers maintain their virtues and character that is judged by their faith by staying together. The small group is used to meet the objective of executing the chosen idea of evangelism and reaching out to those not within the confines of the church. It serves as a tool with an evangelistic purpose. As you begin the process of implementing your small group, here are some helpful if not essential tips and strategies for small group evangelism. While all of them may or may not be applicable to your situation, they are just simple advice when moving forward with an evangelistic small group.

1.   Evangelistic small groups are about building community and sharing faith. Subsequently, they should not become cliques. Your doors should be open to people as long as they are pressing towards the same goal and mission of the small group. If they want to go into a different area, it's OK to start a new small group. There should not be an issue about starting a small group with a different emphasis or goal. That should be encouraged and championed as long as the emphasis or goal doesn't take away from the existing small group. This is not a competition. During the implementation of a small group, one of the strategies

should reflect transparency in the group, allowing people of similar objectives and motives to come together. A small group should always be open to everyone and be welcome to all groups to create a favorable environment for sharing among the members.

2.   Evangelistic Small Groups are about sharing faith. Many people fail to understand how to craft their personal witness into a short two to four minute conversation. It may be advantageous for the small group leader to help individuals craft and share their journey with the group and provide feedback. Sharing is the core objective of a small group. Since a small evangelistic group has a core purpose in sharing among the members about the faith, the leaders should ensure that all members are guided and feel like they are able to share and are part of the group. Through interactions and sharing in the small group, discipleship is created among members, which develops their faith and evangelism. In a compliment to discipleship, practice in evangelism is a follow-up step. The need to pressure the members to reach out to non-believers reflects the development of a small group and presents a chance for its expansion.

3.   Plan with the end in mind. The end goal of the small group is to disciple others and show the love of Christ. It's not for political reasons or to show off people's talents. It is essential that planning with the end in mind takes place throughout the life of the small group. The group should evaluate what was or wasn't done correctly, and modify the group as needed. Often, groups run in 7 or 12 week cycles with one off week for evaluation and planning at the end of every cycle.

4.   Your small group may have a slow start but expect the group to grow! I have never had a small group that did not

start off slowly. Maybe, you will find twelve core people but only six show up to the actual meeting and participate. Don't be discouraged. The small group, if led correctly, will grow. If it does not grow numerically, it will grow spiritually. Great care should be taken to avoid focusing on inward development because it may lead to the decline of a group in the future. Discipleship is another fundamental trait in a small group. The outreach of the small group is a significant strategic move towards growth and assurance for the small group even after the founding members are gone. Also, celebrating the recruitment of members to the faith is essential because it produces a therapeutic effect on the new believer, and it communicates that some progress is evident in the group. The outlay of ministry characterizes outreach evangelism. It develops hearts from bondage to discipleship, establishes small group strategies, and implements small groups with the core aim of outreach evangelism.

5. Use your small group to spawn other groups or interests. If your group is growing, it's ok to split the group. This allows you to not only cover more areas but also perform more evangelistic projects. If there is another need that grows from the small group, it's OK to create a subgroup for that need. For example, a local church may start a small group for women. After the group is growing and solidified, the members may notice that there is a need for a married couples' small group. This may spawn a new small group in which the group members are actually married or engaged couples who seek to strengthen their marriage and perform evangelistic functions together. Strategic running of the small groups ensures the successful accomplishment of the preset objectives and promotes easier running of the group. Development in the small group eventually calls for

other group interests to expand growth in all the aspects of members' lives. The strategy also keeps the evangelical of the small groups and maintains the course of the faith by ensuring the continued spread of religion and conversions of nonbelievers to believers.

6. Developing new leaders should be a strategy that is strictly accepted in the group's development. You must teach others how the group is operated at least in part, so new groups can be developed. Developing leaders is part of discipleship and is healthy in the church environment. Small groups achieve their objective through good leadership. Exemplary leadership and the making of new ambitious leaders with zeal to serve enables the aim of sharing in the group and offers continuity.

CHAPTER 7

SMALL GROUP EVANGELISM CONCLUSIONS

"And what you have heard from me in the presence of many witnesses, commit to faithful men who will be able to teach others also."

2 Timothy 2:2

"By beholding, we become changed!"

2 Timothy 2:2 is a convicting reminder that the goal of utilizing small group evangelism should be to disciple and multiply so that others can grow to maturity. Evangelism has its root in eternity, and the christinas life is squarely focused on Jesus Christ and his soon coming. God compels all those that are his followers to love as

He loves. In loving, God gave his only son that who so ever believed in Him might not perish but have everlasting life. We are called to love our fellow brothers and sisters by extending the love of God to those who have not recognized or experienced it in a saving manner. In short, we share the gospel because we love like God loves and do not wish that anyone should perish or be unaware. Jesus provides the great commission to His disciples that not only challenges us to make disciples, baptize and teach but also promises power and authority to carry out the command with the power of the Holy Spirit. In essence Jesus not only gives us the command but the tools to carry out the command convicting His followers of its importance. Furthermore, we see in Acts 2:42-47 that the expectations of every member of the community of believers. Their devotion was not only to learning and teaching about God but fellowship and togetherness that when others saw, they immediately joined.

As part of our conviction, we understand that lost people do not willingly glorify or submit to God or Jesus Christ. God created the world to display His glory (psalm 19) and frm the foundation of its existence knew that man would fall and supplied a redeemer. We are to be co-laborers, under the power of the Holy Spirit working to reach those that have not yet entered into a saving relationship with Jesus Christ. Utilizing small group evangelism is important because it provides the vehicle to not only display the love of Christ and reach new people who may possibly become believers but also to develop the character and relationships of those who have already know their Lord and savior. By being inclusive and promoting "love and good works" as found in Hebrews 10:24-25, the evangelistic small group becomes an encouragement to each other and draw closer together.

Utilizing small group evangelism is essential in the growing of today's church. In a recent survey of the fastest growing churches in North America, thier pastors credited small group evangelism with their success. By implementing small group evangelism congregations were able to grow quickly and church membership involvement greatly increased. While people may have a different idea on what constitutes small group evangelism, the simple fact that all agree on is that they are a powerful tool that can be utilized to fulfill our mission and hasten the soon coming of our Lord and Savior, Jesus Christ! Small group evangelism changes lives! People get an opportunity to experience a real relationship with each other and Jesus. They are strengthened, enlightened and sanctified by the Holy Spirit. Spirits will be renewed, and souls will be added daily. If I can implore you to anything in your ministry, its to develop and start small groups that are appropriate in your context and use them as vehicles of ministry.

Chapter 8

Example Plan For Small Group Evangelism

Beloved, if God so loved us, we also ought to love one another. No one has ever seen God; if we love one another, God abides in us and his love is perfected in us. By this we know that we abide in him and he in us, because he has given us of his Spirit.

1 John 4:11-13 ESV

"Love, then love some more!"

The below plan is simply an example plan that could be used to jumpstart your small group. While this plan is meant to be enacted as part of the local congregation, it does not have to be limited to that scope. It simply could be started as a side project by any Christian group that is operating from a home.

PARTICIPANTS

Participants should be selected based upon the group's needs. Groups should consider inviting couples, men, and people from a desired age group. Additionally, they should have a desired number of members in mind. In the example, our participants will be members of the same church with a maximum starting number of twelve members. The ages of the participants are of no consequence; however, because transportation may be an issue, and the group seeks to add younger adults , the specified participants will be between the ages of eighteen to fifty. While more than the twelve core members may start attending the functions and grow the small group, the starting group is limited to the twelve individuals. Start recruiting your participants. Make them aware of the goal or mission of the small group and ask them to commit themselves to the initial first run which will be a thirteen-week process. Call each participant and confirm the initial meeting time, place, and location.

GATHERING AND EVENTS

The small group example has a commitment to both personal community gatherings and weekly evangelistic events over a thirteen-week period. There will be two weekly meetings. The first meeting will be a core group gathering to build community and discuss evangelism. These meetings will take place on Saturday afternoons and will be scheduled in either the church fellowship hall or a participant's home. At the community meeting, participants will share a full meal including an entrée, refreshments, and snacks. Multiple options will be made available for those who have specific dietary concerns. After eating, the core curriculum will be taught to emphasize evangelism in the attendees' lives. After the first meeting, new individuals will be able to join the core team meeting. This meeting will take approximately two hours for the meal and the presentation of the curriculum.

The second meeting will be a community outreach event. The outreach events are designed to take the small group out into the community to evangelize and assist in particular community-based efforts. The end goal is to allow people to work towards the good of others and share their faith while working as part of a small group. The outreach events will occur on Thursdays or Sundays, and usually, they will last for two to three hours. These events can be planned and executed by the small group leader or by a third party with whom the group is working. For example, this work can include working in a soup kitchen that is already established or performing a Toys for Tots drive. Even if they are a part of a greater effort, the group will attempt to stay together as much as possible.

Within the thirteen weeks, there will be a total of twenty-six meetings and a conclusion worship service that occurs at the church. The total order and goals of the twenty-six meetings are to talk about a specific topic, which in our example, is personal evangelism and perform one act of community service per week. Below is an outline you can adapt to your group:

WEEK 1: The goal for week one is to discuss the goals of the training group, its schedule, and the obligations for each meeting. The group's aim is to learn the ideas and skills to do small group evangelism, to develop a warm, caring group to encourage outreach, and to participate in all weekly group events.

Small Group Gathering: Saturday at fellowship hall directly after service.

i.   Meal (45 Minutes)
ii. Introduction (5 Minutes)

iii.   Getting to Know One Another (30 minutes): Provide name and answer and ice breaker question that will be provided.

iv.   Principles of Evangelism (40 minutes): Talk about the topics below:

1.   Great Commission
2.   Every member is a minister
3.   God's role in evangelism
4.   Hopes and fears of evangelism
5.   Outreach Event: Thursday 6PM-8PM

v.   Food Pantry Food Distribution

WEEK 2: Continue to develop group dynamics as well as have each member identify his or her spiritual gifts and share how those gifts can be effective in evangelism.

Small Group Gathering: Saturday at fellowship hall directly after service

i.   Meal (45 Minutes)
ii.   Introduction (5 Minutes)
iii.   Spiritual Gifts

1.   Introduction (5 minutes)
2.   Principles of Spiritual gifts (20 minutes)
3.   Spiritual Gifts and Evangelism (20 minutes)
4.   Spiritual Gifts Survey and Scoring (60 minutes)
5.   Concluding Remarks (15 minutes)

iv.   Outreach Event: Thursday 6PM-8PM

i.   Food Pantry Food Distribution

WEEK 3: This week will be focused on witnessing. Members need to understand the principles of inviting someone to Christ and developing their own personal testimony that they can share.

Small Group Gathering: Saturday at fellowship hall directly after service

    i.   Meal (45 Minutes)
    ii.   Introduction (5 Minutes)
    iii. Witnessing

        1.   Introduction (5 minutes)
        2.   Principles of invitation (20 minutes)
        3.   What is my witness (20 minutes)
        4.   Developing your witness story and invitation (60 minutes)
        5.   Concluding Remarks (15 minutes)

    iv.   Outreach Event: Thursday 6PM-8PM

        i.   Food Pantry Food Distribution

WEEK 4: This week will be about learning how to share and listen to others and their life experiences, how to share personally what they are experiencing, and how to hear and encourage others by providing feedback without judgment.

Small Group Gathering: Saturday at fellowship hall directly after service

    i.   Meal (45 Minutes)
    ii.   Introduction (5 Minutes)
    iii. Christian conversation

        1.   Introduction (5 minutes)
        2.   Listening Exercise (20 minutes)

    3.   Caring Exercise (20 minutes)
    4.   Sharing Exercise (60 minutes)
    5.   Concluding Remarks (15 minutes)

  iv.   Outreach Event: Thursday 6PM-8PM

    i.   Food Pantry Food Distribution

WEEK 5: This week focuses on what prayer is, how to intercede on someone's behalf, and what group prayer is. At the end, the small group will choose and plan an activity to perform during Week 9 that is of interest to the group.

Small Group Gathering: Saturday at fellowship hall directly after service

  i.   Meal (45 Minutes)
  ii.   Introduction (5 Minutes)
  iii.   Prayer and planning

    1.   Introduction (5 minutes)
    2.   Principles of Prayer (20 minutes)
    3.   Group Prayer (20 minutes)
    4.   Planning Outreach Event(s) (60 minutes)
    5.   Concluding Remarks (15 minutes)

  iv.   Outreach Event: Thursday 6PM-8PM

    i.   Food Pantry Food Distribution

WEEK 6: During this week the small group will put prayer as a group into practice. Then, they will spend a small amount of time talking about the group and the way things are going thus far. Finally, they will plan an outreach activity to perform during week 10.

Small Group Gathering: Saturday at fellowship hall directly after service

    i.   Meal (45 Minutes)
    ii.   Introduction (5 Minutes)
    iii. Prayer, Process and Plan

        1.   Introduction (5 minutes)
        2.   Group Prayer (20 minutes)
        3.   Discuss the Group (20 minutes)
        4.   Plan Outreach Events (60 minutes)
        5.   Concluding Remarks (15 minutes)

    iv.   Outreach Event: Thursday 6PM-8PM

        i.   Food Pantry Food Distribution

WEEK 7: During this week, the group will seek to get a better understanding of Jesus and the gospel. They will learn why His death and resurrection are good news and why those events are important? They will explore what He accomplished specifically and how it is both corporate and personal.

Small Group Gathering: Saturday at fellowship hall directly after service

    i.   Meal (45 Minutes)
    ii.   Introduction (5 Minutes)
    iii. Evaluation (10 minutes)
    iv.   Who is Jesus to me?

        1.   Introduction (5 minutes)
        2.   Who is Jesus in the Bible? (10 minutes)
        3.   What did Jesus accomplish? (15 minutes)
        4.   Why is that important? (10 minutes)

     5.   Making Jesus Personal (15)

     6.   Concluding Remarks (5 minutes)

  v.   Outreach Event: Thursday 6PM-8PM

     i.   Food Pantry Food Distribution

WEEK 8: This week is about discussing how they can enter into a relationship with Jesus Christ and what has changed. The goal is to get people to see that while the members of the group have relationships with God, those relationships can mean different things.

Small Group Gathering: Saturday at fellowship hall directly after service

    i.   Meal (45 Minutes)
    ii.   Introduction (5 Minutes)
   iii.   Personal Journey

     1.   Introduction (5 minutes)
     2.   How did you get to know Christ? (40 minutes)
     3.   What can you say about that to others? (20 minutes)
     4.   Concluding Remarks (5 minutes)

   iv.   Outreach Event: Thursday 6PM-8PM

     i.   Food Pantry Food Distribution

WEEK 9: This week is about praying and discussing the group. Two-thirds of the research project is now complete. What has been accomplished? How does everyone feel? What still needs to be done?

Another planning session will take place to discuss an outreach event for Week 11 of the group's choosing.

Small Group Gathering: Saturday at fellowship hall directly after service

    i.   Meal (45 Minutes)
    ii.   Introduction (5 Minutes)
    iii. Prayer, Process and Plan II

        1.   Introduction (5 minutes)
        2.   Group Prayer (20 minutes)
        3.   Discuss the Group (20 minutes)
        4.   Plan Outreach Events (60 minutes)
        5.   Concluding Remarks (15 minutes)

    iv. Outreach Event: Thursday 6PM-8PM

        i.   Provided by group from Week 5.

WEEK 10: The goal of this week is to shift to a book that is focused on Christ. The study and emphasis will be on Chapter 1 of the book, *Steps to Christ,* that expounds upon the idea of God's love for man. (He sent his only begotten Son, etc.)

Small Group Gathering: Saturday at fellowship hall directly after service

    i.   Meal (45 Minutes)
    ii.   Introduction (5 Minutes)
    iii. *Steps to Christ* Book Chapter 1

        1.   Introduction (5 minutes)
        2.   Group Prayer (10 minutes)
        3.   Discuss the Book (45 minutes)
        4.   Concluding Remarks (10 minutes)

    iv.   Outreach Event: Thursday 6PM-8PM

        i.   Provided by the group from Week 6.

WEEK 11: The goal of this week is to continue the group study on the book, *Steps to Christ*. Chapter 2 expounds on the concept of sinners who are in need of Christ.

Small Group Gathering: Saturday at fellowship hall directly after service

    i.   Meal (45 Minutes)
    ii.   Introduction (5 Minutes)
    iii.   *Steps to Christ* Chapter 2

        1.   Introduction (5 minutes)
        2.   Group Prayer (10 minutes)
        3.   Discuss the Book (45 minutes)
        4.   Concluding Remarks (10 minutes)

    iv.   Outreach Event: Thursday 6PM-8PM

        i.   Provided by the group from Week 9.

WEEK 12: The goal of this week is to continue the group study on the book, *Steps to Christ*. Chapter 3 discusses repentance.

Small Group Gathering: Saturday at fellowship hall directly after service

    i.   Meal (45 Minutes)
    ii.   Introduction (5 Minutes)
    iii.   *Steps to Christ* Chapter 3

        1.   Introduction (5 minutes)
        2.   Group Prayer (10 minutes)

      3.   Discuss the Book (45 minutes)

      4.   Concluding Remarks (10 minutes)

  iv.   Outreach Event: Thursday 6PM-8PM

      i.   Food Pantry Food Distribution

WEEK 13: The goal of this week is to finalize the group's activities, take surveys, and give comments, suggestions, etc. Invite everyone to the following week's worship service to celebrate and plan for future small group sessions.

Small Group Gathering: Saturday at fellowship hall directly after service

  i.   Meal (45 Minutes)

  ii.   Introduction (5 Minutes)

  iii.   What's Next?

      1.   Introduction (5 minutes)

      2.   Group Prayer (10 minutes)

      3.   Discuss the Group and Surveys (10 minutes)

      4.   Plan What's Next (60 minutes)

      5.   Concluding Remarks (5 minutes)

  iv.   Outreach Event: Thursday 6PM-8PM

      i.   Food Pantry Food Distribution

  v.   Sabbath Worship

      i.   Congratulate and replicate results

At the culmination or conclusion to the thirteen-week session will be a "Friends and Family" service held at the church. During this service's worship program, individuals will be recognized for their achievement and participation in the thirteen-week session. All individuals involved will be recognized including the core team, people who joined the effort, and those who may have participated in response to the efforts of the team.

About the Author

Dr. John R. Sconiers, II, DMin, is a senior pastor, preacher, mentor, and evangelism coordinator. His education includes DMin in evangelism and church planting, DIT in Security, MAPM (MDIV Equivalent), MIS, as well as postgraduate work in counseling. He also holds numerous certifications and has hosted training sessions. Dr. Sconiers has lived and preached in various parts of the world and has a passion for seeing lives transformed by the power of the Holy Spirit and seeks to point others to the good news of Jesus Christ. Dr. Sconiers currently serves as a senior pastor in the North Georgia area. He is married to one wife, Nicole, and they share five amazing children.

Connect with Dr. Sconiers

You can connect with Dr. John R Sconiers II via:

Instagram: @johnsconiers

Twitter: @johnsconiers

YouTube: @JohnSconiers

Email: John@realmomentsmedia.com

Website: http://www.johnsconiers2.com